D1050058

1

The Young Scientist's Guide to

SUCCESSFUL SCIENCE PROJECTS

The Young Scientist's Guide to

SUCCESSFUL SCIENCE PROJECTS

by SANDRA MARKLE

Illustrations by MARTI SHOHET

A BEECH TREE PAPERBACK BOOK
NEW YORK

ACKNOWLEDGMENTS

The author wishes to say a special thank-you to Peter Forde, Advanced Genetic Sciences, and George Watchmaker, Lawrence Livermore National Laboratory, for their assistance.

5 6 7 8 9 10 11 12

Library of Congress Cataloging in Publication Data
Markle, Sandra.
The young scientist's guide to successful science projects / by Sandra Markle ; illustrations by Marti Shohet.   p.   cm.   Summary: Experiments and investigations to teach necessary skills and prepare one for choosing a science project. ISBN 0-688-09137-7
1. Science projects—Handbooks, manuals, etc.
—Juvenile litearature.   [1. Science projects.   2. Experiments.]   I. Shohet, Marti, ill.
II. Title.   Q182.3.M37   1989   507.8—dc20
89-45290   CIP   AC

Contents

For curious kids everywhere,
and especially for
Brian Clack, Holly Markle,
Kalani Sylva, and Laniq Thornton.

Introduction

So you've decided to do a science project. Maybe you enjoy the fun of investigating things. Maybe you want to enter a science fair. Or maybe you need to do a project for school. Whatever your reason, you might now be asking yourself, "What topic should I pick for my science project?" Before you can answer that question, you need to know what the parts of a science project are. And you need to know how to design and conduct a successful science experiment.

Sound hard? It won't be when you work in order through the chapters in this book. Step-by-step you'll learn the skills you need. Then, equipped with those skills, you'll be ready to find a topic for your science project. And you'll also know how to set up the project you select.

Don't get too comfortable, though. You're not just going to be reading about how to do a science project. This book is packed with hands-on investigations to keep you actively involved each step of the way.

Ready? Then don't wait another minute. Turn the page and let's get started.

STEP 1

Learning What a Science Project Is

Set an empty plastic milk jug next to an empty plastic bottle that once contained soda pop and compare them. You'll see that the jug is cloudy and the bottle is clear. The bottle feels tougher when you poke it. The reason for these differences is that the plastics used to make the two containers are different. Why?

Until a few years ago, soda pop came only in glass bottles and metal cans. Plastic bottles would have been cheaper to produce and lighter to ship and store, but soft-drink bottlers found that plastic bottles didn't keep the bubbles in soda pop.

Carbonated drinks, like soda pop, contain carbon dioxide gas. That's the gas that gives these drinks their familiar fizz. When it is added to a liquid and the liquid is sealed under pressure, the carbon dioxide gas remains suspended in the liquid. Because it is invisible, you can't tell it's there. But as

11

soon as the container is opened and the pressure lessened, the carbon dioxide gas begins to escape in the form of bubbles.

To see this, look through the side of an unopened clear bottle of soda pop. You won't see any bubbles in the liquid. Then remove the cap, which releases the pressure, and look again. This time you'll see lots of tiny bubbles.

Nathaniel Wyeth, a mechanical engineer, wondered why drinks in plastic bottles lost their fizz. He wanted to see for himself what happened when soda pop was stored in a plastic container. After filling a clean plastic milk jug with ginger ale, he capped it and put it into the refrigerator. Within a few hours, the jug was so swollen he could barely pry it out from between the refrigerator shelves.

Wyeth realized that the plastic wasn't strong enough to keep the soda pop under pressure. To solve this problem, he experimented, trying different techniques he hoped would increase the plastic's strength. At last, Wyeth discovered that stretching plastic made it stronger—strong enough to hold under pressure the liquid it contained. So Wyeth reported his discovery, and it revolutionized the bottling industry.

What Nathaniel Wyeth presented was a science project. Your project may or may not have such a dramatic effect on an industry. You will accomplish it, however, by taking the same three steps Nathaniel Wyeth did when he solved the problem of storing carbonated drinks in plastic.

First, you'll identify a problem that needs to be solved. Next, you'll conduct an experiment. And then you'll make a presentation. You may have an opportunity to talk about your experiment. But it is more likely that you'll make a display with pictures, graphs (which you'll learn about later), and lists of information to help explain your work and accomplishments.

Your display will tell the story of what you did and what you discovered in your experiment. The key part of your science project will be the experiment you conducted. So before you can decide what problem to try to solve by experimenting, you need to know what a science experiment is. The answer to that is coming up next.

Understanding What
an Experiment Is

The best way to find out about experimenting is to *do* an experiment. The chance to experiment is what's really fun aboout doing a science project. So try this experiment.

You will need a sponge, a magazine, a clock with a second hand, some water, a ruler, a sheet of notebook paper, and a friend to help you. Then follow these directions:

First, soak the sponge in water and squeeze it out so that it is wet but not dripping.

Next, press the sponge down on a sheet of paper, on a tabletop or against a chalkboard to leave a wet spot, and quickly measure the length of this spot. Write down your first measurement. Wait one minute. Then, recheck and record the length of the wet spot again.

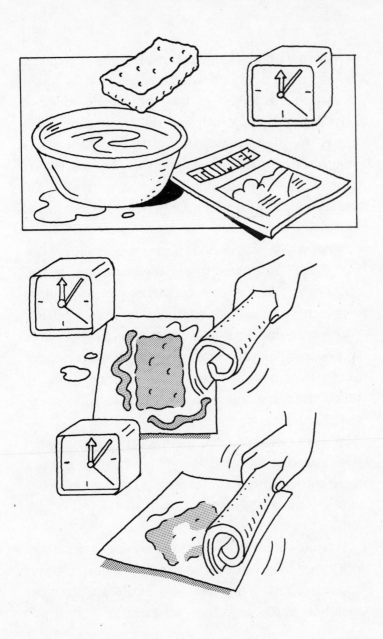

Now, wet the sponge again, squeeze it out, and make a fresh wet spot. This time, as soon as you've measured the length of this spot, begin to fan it very slowly. Have your friend signal when one minute is up. Then, remeasure and record the spot's length. Finally, make and measure one more wet spot. What you'll do differently *this* time is to fan the spot rapidly for one minute before remeasuring its length.

What you've just done is to test the statement that *the greater the wind speed, the faster water will evaporate.* Did the measurements you took make you believe that the statement is true, or false? To be sure that what you observed is likely to happen every time, you would need to repeat the entire test at least two more times and average your results (averaging is something you'll learn to do in step 7).

At this point, however, the important thing is that you've discovered what an experiment is. It is a test done to determine a relationship between two factors—in this case, between wind speed and evaporation.

You may be wondering how you decide what factors to test. And you may be wondering how to come up with a test. If so, then you're already thinking ahead to *designing* an experiment of your own.

16

Reading about other experiments and *analyzing* them (something you'll find out more about as we go along) are good ways to figure out the basic parts you'll want to include when you design your own science project. And that's what you'll do in step 3.

STEP 3

Recognizing the Parts of a Typical Experiment

To design a science experiment, you need to be able to identify the four main parts that make up any typical experiment—the *controlled variables,* the *manipulated variable,* the *responding variable,* and the *hypothesis.* You're probably thinking, "Hey, I don't even know what those words mean." To help you learn what the words mean and learn to recognize those parts of an experiment, let's take a closer look at a science experiment. Suppose you want to test whether it's true that the more water a plant receives, the taller it gets. Let's write that down as a statement: *As the amount of water plants receive increases, their overall height also increases.*

You could test this situation by watering several plants and not watering several others. However, if the plants used weren't all the same kind, the results wouldn't be very useful. The plants you watered could just naturally grow taller than the ones you didn't water.

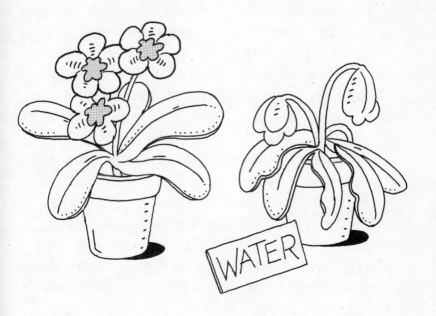

It probably seems obvious that the plants you're testing should all be the same kind. But what would it do to your experiment if all the plants were the same kind, but you put some of them in big pots and others in small pots? Or if some of the plants were placed in full sun while others were in the shade? Under any of these conditions, you couldn't be sure that a plant's growth—or lack of growth—had anything to do with the amount of water it received.

Now you can see one of the problems in an experiment. Often there are a lot of factors that can

19

influence the results. Scientists call such factors *variables*. When you experiment, you want to test the effect of one particular variable. That variable is called the *manipulated variable* because you are manipulating it—or changing it—in some specific way. In the experiment we are analyzing now, for example, water is the manipulated variable.

The change you are watching for is called the *responding variable*. In this case, it is the height of the plants. All the other variables—sunlight, pot size, and the type of plant—need to be kept from affecting the responding variable. In an experiment, those variables that are kept from having an effect on the results are said to be controlled and are called *controlled variables*.

In other words, to find out what effect the manipulated variable (water) has on the responding variable (plant growth), you must make certain that the controlled variables (amount of light, size of pot, kind of plant) are the same.

Let's see if you can identify the variables in this experiment. First, look at the picture showing an experiment being started. Then, see if you can name at least four variables that are being controlled. Write these down on a sheet of notebook paper so you can check yourself by reading the answers that follow.

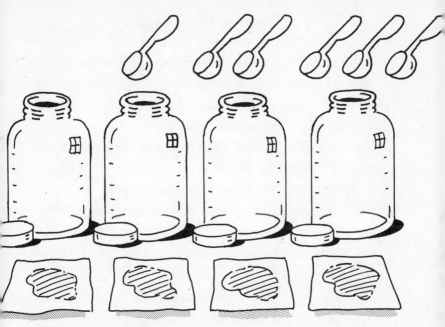

Did you spot these variables being controlled?
1. Amount of water
2. Size and shape of the container
3. Size of cloth square
4. Type of cloth
5. Size and type of stain on the cloth
6. Lids for the containers

You may have thought of other variables that could be called controlled, too, such as water temperature and exposure to sunlight. Just remember: All the variables other than the one being manipulated need to be controlled in an experiment. The amount of detergent added is the variable being manipulated in this experiment. Did you pick out the responding variable—the one being measured? If you said how much of the stain is removed or how clean the cloth becomes, you're right!

OK—you're off to a great start. Here's another chance for you to practice identifying the variables in an experiment. Look at the pictures as you read the directions for conducting the experiment. Next, list all the variables you can find that are being controlled. Then, write down which one variable is being manipulated. Finally, record which responding variable is being measured. Check yourself by reading the answers. (In this experiment and throughout the book, we're using the metric system. You'll find out why in step 6.)

1. To make an electromagnet, you'll need a 6-volt lantern battery, 50 centimeters of insulated copper wire, a 4- to 5-inch nail, and scissors. First, strip 2.5 centimeters of insulation off each end of the wire and attach a bare end to each terminal of the battery to switch the magnet on.
2. To test the electromagnet's strength, see how many standard-size steel paper clips the wire can pick up. Repeat this test two times.
3. Next, unhook one end of the wire from the battery, wind it around the nail ten times to form ten coils, slip the nail out, and reattach the end

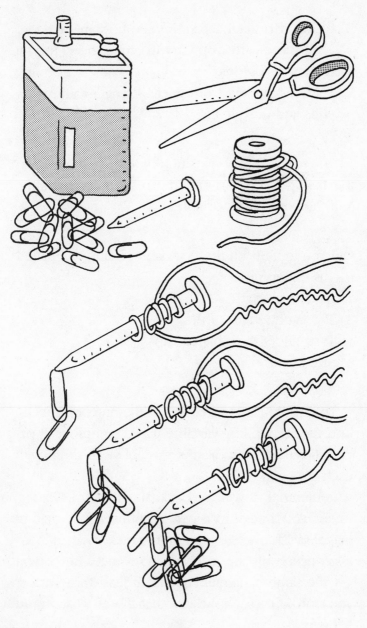

of the wire to the battery. See how many paper clips the electromagnet will attract now. Repeat the test as before.

4. Then test the electromagnet's strength with twenty coils and thirty coils.

Don't read ahead now until you've written down the manipulated variable, the responding variable, and the controlled variables.

Did you identify all these variables being controlled in this experiment?

1. Battery strength
2. Type and length of the wire
3. Type and size of paper clips
4. Size of the coils

The manipulated variable was the number of coils. And the responding variable was the number of paper clips the electromagnet was able to pick up with each set of coils.

Remember, if you were actually doing this experiment, you'd need to repeat each test of the manipulated variable at least two more times. What happens just once could be a freak occurrence. But if you get the same or similar results at least three times, you can be reasonably sure that this is what would happen every time.

Ready for a bigger challenge? Then imagine a very moldy piece of bread. Pretend that you want to do an experiment to test whether a colder-than-normal environment will affect how quickly mold forms. The manipulated variable is temperature. The responding variable will be the first signs of fuzzy green mold growing on the bread. On a piece of notebook paper, write down all the variables you can think of that you would need to control to do this test. Then, check yourself by reading the answers on page 27.

"Whoa!" you're probably thinking. "How am I supposed to think of every variable that could change? I don't even know what steps will be done in the experiment."

Well, you may not think of *all* the variables that need to be controlled. But if you tackle this problem in an organized way, you will have a good chance of coming close. Divide your paper into two columns. Write a heading at the top of one column with the name of the test object—in this case, BREAD—and put at the top of the other column ENVIRONMENT, the heading that refers to such variables as sunlight and air.

When you're trying to think of all the environmental factors that could have an effect, it may help you to know there's a set of variables that should always be considered. You may want to keep this list handy to check anytime you experiment:

1. Exposure to sunlight
2. Air movement (wind and drafts)
3. Air temperature
4. Amount of water in the air (relative humidity)

However, in the experiment about mold growth, air temperature is not the manipulated variable. It would be on the list of controlled variables for that particular experiment.

Next, try to think of all the things about the bread

that could affect the growth of mold. You may want to visit the library and read in books and encyclopedias about bread. Understanding your subject will help you think of variables that could affect it. You may want to find out more about mold, too. PRESERVATIVES, which slow the growth of mold, is a variable you might list in the BREAD column.

Did you identify these variables that need to be controlled? You may have listed even more.

Bread
1. Preservatives
2. Thickness of slice
3. Amount of sugar in recipe

Environment
1. Size of container
2. Exposure to air movement
3. Exposure to sunlight
4. Amount of moisture in the air

Ready for your biggest challenge so far? Look at the experiment setup showing containers filled with soil. On a sheet of notebook paper, write down what variable you think is being manipulated. Then, tell what the responding variable is in this experiment. Finally, list all the variables that need to be controlled.

Be careful! Not all the variables that need to be controlled are visible in the picture. Check yourself by looking at the answers.

27

Here are the answers. How did you do?

Manipulated variable: Size of the soil particles.

Responding variable: How much water drains through. (You could include a time limit on the responding variable, such as how much water drains through in one minute.)

Controlled variables:

Test object	*Environment*
1. Size of container	1. Exposure to sunlight
2. Shape of container	2. Air temperature
3. Type of soil	3. Air movement
4. Amount of water added	

As you may have guessed from the photographs, the easiest way to be sure that you've controlled all the variables that need to be kept the same is to prepare several identical setups. Treat all the setups exactly the same except for the one variable that you are manipulating.

So far, you've learned to recognize the manipulated variable, the responding variable, and the controlled variables. The one remaining part of a typical science experiment that you have yet to explore is the *hypothesis.*

An experiment is done to find out what effect the manipulated variable has on the responding variable. So a typical experiment starts with a statement of what you expect to happen. You are actually making sort of a guess about the relationship between those two variables. For example, you could begin an experiment with this statement: *The colder it is, the slower seeds sprout.* That statement of the supposed relationship between the manipulated and responding variables is a *hypothesis*. You don't know if it's true. It isn't a statement of fact. It's a guess, but it's an important guess because it guides you to set up the experiment in a way that proves whether the statement is in fact true or false.

You must be wondering, "How do I choose a manipulated variable and a responding variable for the hypothesis?" And you must be curious about how to guess at the relationship between those two variables. Those decisions are so important that learning how to construct a hypothesis is a whole separate step—step 4.

STEP 4

Constructing a Hypothesis

There won't be any sweet treats from strawberry blossoms that have been destroyed by frost. But strawberries aren't the only plant to suffer from late frosts. Government reports show that in the United States alone, frost causes about $1.6 billion worth of crop damage every year.

If you're wondering whether something can be done to protect plants from frost, you're on your way to constructing a hypothesis and performing an experiment.

You probably wonder about different things you hear or see each day at home, in school, or on TV. So it may not surprise you that nine-tenths of all science experiments start when somebody gets curious about, or thinks of, a responding variable that he or she would like to observe. For example, in the story about the frost-damaged crops, researchers wanted to do an experiment in which they could measure the number of plants that *resisted* frost and remained healthy. What they needed to find was a manipulating variable—something to test—that would keep frost from forming on sensitive plants.

It is easy to construct a hypothesis if you first come up with a list of variables that could affect the responding variable. You probably remember from step 3 that these variables fall into two groups: those that affect the object in the responding variable and those that affect the object's environment.

As you did in the problem of the moldy bread, make a list of variables that might affect how well plants resist frost damage. Once again, divide a sheet of notebook paper into two columns. Name one column PLANTS and the other ENVIRONMENT. Next, ask yourself what characteristics of a plant might affect whether it will be damaged by frost. It's a good idea to visit the library and read more about plants and plant growth while you're tackling this challenge. List these variables in the PLANTS column. Then consider what environmental conditions might affect whether frost forms on plants and list these in the ENVIRONMENT column. When you've finished, check yourself by reading the answer coming up next.

These are only some of the possible variables:

Plants
1. Age of plant
2. Amount of exposed leaf area

Environment
1. Air temperature
2. Wind speed
3. Amount of moisture in the air

A hypothesis needs to point the way toward the steps that will be taken in the experiment. When you state a hypothesis, make it show in what way the manipulated variable will be changed, then tell what effect you think this will have on the responding variable. For the problem of preventing frost damage, you could construct this hypothesis: *As the age of the plant increases, the resistance to frost damage also increases.* Or you could state: *As the air temperature decreases, the amount of frost damage increases.*

Choosing words like *decrease* and *increase* or *faster* and *slower* shows the way you think the manipulated variable will need to change in the test. Those words are your way of predicting what relationship you expect to observe between the manipulated and responding variables. You could also use such words as *bigger* and *smaller, higher* and *lower,* or *more* and *less.*

Okay, it's your turn to construct hypotheses (the plural of hypothesis). Look back at the list of possible manipulated variables in the PLANTS and ENVI-RONMENT columns. Then write a hypothesis for each one. Remember, the responding variable is the amount of frost damage. When you've finished, check yourself by reading the answers.

Here are some possible hypotheses. Yours may be worded differently and still be correct, as long as each hypothesis shows in what way the manipulated variable will change and predicts what effect that change will have on the responding variable.

1. As the amount of exposed leaf area *decreases,* the amount of frost damage *decreases.*
2. The *more steadily* the wind blows, the *less* frost damage occurs.
3. As the amount of moisture in the air *increases,* the amount of frost damage also *increases.*

OK—it's time to put your new abilities to the test. Look at the problem pictured below. First, identify the responding variable. Next, list all the manipulating variables. Then construct at least three hypotheses that could be used to test the relationship between these manipulating variables and the responding variable. Check yourself by reading the answers that follow.

The problem is: *Why do some batches of popped*

corn have more duds (unpopped kernels) than others?

Did you recognize that the responding variable was the number of unpopped kernels in a batch? These are possible manipulated variables that could affect that responding variable. (You may have thought of others.)

1. Size of individual kernels
2. Dryness of kernels
3. Length of time stored
4. Temperature during popping
5. Amount of moisture in the air

Remember, your hypotheses don't have to be worded the same as the ones listed below to be correct.

1. As the size of the kernels increases, the number of unpopped kernels in a batch increases.
2. The drier the kernels, the more unpopped kernels will be present in a batch.
3. The longer the popcorn has been stored, the more unpopped kernels will be present in a batch.
4. As the popping temperature decreases, the number of unpopped kernels per batch increases.
5. As the amount of moisture in the air increases, the number of unpopped kernels decreases.

To finish this challenge, try listing all the variables that would need to be controlled if you were doing an experiment to test the first hypothesis. Then, check yourself by reading the answers written below.

Did you identify that these variables need to be controlled? Did you think of others?

1. Type of popcorn
2. Size of popper
3. Number of kernels in a batch
4. Temperature of popper
5. Moisture in the air
6. Dryness of kernels
7. Length of time kernels were stored

So far you've learned how to construct the framework of an experiment. You've learned to spot the manipulated variable, the responding variable, and the controlled variables. You've also learned how to state a hypothesis that shows a relationship between the manipulated and responding variables. And you know you can create a testable situation. Now, you're ready to design and set up the test.

But first, a word about logbooks. It's time to assemble yours. Scientists record what they do and what results they observe each time they experiment. They also keep a written account—carefully dated and periodically signed by witnesses—to prove just when they made each discovery. It can be crucial for a scientist filing for a patent (legal rights to an invention) to prove he or she was first to have an idea or to make a discovery.

Your logbook is your record of what you do as you plan and perform your experiment. At some point, it will become part of your project's display. A three-ring binder would make a good logbook. Or you could hook together a stack of notebook paper with paper clips, staples, or paper fasteners. Your logbook should have a cover and a page for each of the following:

1. The hypothesis
2. List of variables: manipulated variable, responding variable, and controlled variable
3. Procedure
4. List of supplies and equipment
5. Data table
6. Observations
7. Graph
8. Conclusion

Granted, you don't know how to do *all* these things yet. But we'll go through it—step-by-step.

STEP 5

Designing an Experiment

Ready for a snack? Then here's a quick, healthful treat you can make:

Peanut-Butter Bumbles

You'll need a bowl, crunchy peanut butter, powdered milk, honey, a measuring cup, a spoon, a tablespoon, a bag of coconut, and waxed paper.

Directions:

1. Mix together 2 cups peanut butter, 1 cup powdered milk, and 4 tablespoons of honey.
2. Pour about a cup of coconut out on a sheet of waxed paper.
3. Scoop out a heaping tablespoon of the peanut butter mixture, roll it into a ball with your hands and roll the ball in the coconut. Repeat, pouring out more coconut as needed, until you've used up all the peanut-butter mixture.

Think you could follow the directions to prepare Peanut-Butter Bumbles without any more instructions from anyone? Sure you could! The instructions are complete, simple, and take you step-by-step through the process.

That's exactly what the set of directions for your experiment design needs to be—complete, simple to follow, step-by-step. Scientists call it the *procedure*. It will be, first of all, a set of directions for you to follow as you collect data—or information—about whether or not the hypothesis you wrote is true. But your procedure should be written so clearly that someone else could easily repeat your experiment. That's good scientific method. The more often a test is done, the better. And scientists often duplicate the experiments of other scientists to find out if they can get the same or nearly the same results.

The easiest way to write an experiment's procedure is to divide the job into three parts:

1. Describe how to change the manipulated variable, making it clear what values (numerical or otherwise) that variable will have.
2. Tell how to measure the responding variable.
3. Describe what should be done to control the other variables.

To help you learn how to write these three parts of the procedure, read through how it is done in this example. The hypothesis is: *As the temperature increases, the amount of carbon dioxide that bubbles out of soda pop increases.*

Procedure:
(Describe how to change the manipulated variable, making it clear what values that variable will have.)
1. Collect five unopened plastic bottles of the same size of one brand of soda pop. Set each of them in identical containers that are larger than the bottles. Use masking tape and a marking pen to label these containers 1 through 5.
2. Next, figure out how many cups of water will need to be poured into each container to nearly cover the sides of the soda-pop bottle. Measure the water and pour exactly the same amount into each container. Use a thermometer to make sure the water poured into the first container is 10°C. Mark this temperature on the masking tape. The water poured into the other four containers should be, respectively, 20°C, 30°C, 40°C, and 50°C. Label each of these temperatures on the corresponding masking-tape labels.
3. Take off the bottle caps and immediately cover the top of each bottle with the neck of one of five identical, large round rubber balloons. Have a friend help, if necessary, so that the balloons are on the five bottles as close to the same time as possible.

(Tell how to measure the responding variable.)
4. Use a measuring tape or a string and a ruler to measure the diameter of each balloon at its biggest point after one minute has passed, then again after two minutes have passed, and once more after three minutes. Record this information on a chart.
5. Repeat the entire test three times.
(All the directions to keep things—containers, balloons, etc.—the same are designed to control the other variables that could have an effect on the results.)

The manipulated variable in this experiment was temperature. What were the values of the manipulated variable in the procedure? And what technique was used to expose the test bottles of soda pop to each of those temperatures?

The responding variable was the amount of carbon dioxide gas that escaped from the soda pop. A scientist working in a laboratory might have a special instrument designed to collect the escaping gas and measure it. But you won't have that kind of equipment. You'll need to be creative. You need to think of familiar, easy-to-find, free or inexpensive equipment that you can use to do the job. This procedure suggested that balloons could be used to catch the escaping gas and that a measuring tape would provide some idea of how much captured carbon dioxide gas was in the balloons.

What variables were controlled in this experiment? Five identical setups would help ensure that only temperature would be changed. Did you notice that a friend is needed to help with the variable that's the most difficult to control: opening the bottles of soda pop at as nearly the same moment as possible?

OK, now that you know what to look for, try this challenge. Read through this experiment's hypothesis and procedure. Then, answer each of these questions on a sheet of notebook paper:

1. In what way was the manipulated variable changed and what values did it have in this experiment?
2. How was the responding variable measured?
3. What variables were being controlled?

Check yourself by reading the answers on the next two pages.

The hypothesis is: *As the thickness of the insulation increases, the amount of heat loss decreases.*

Procedure:

1. Cut ten 15-centimeter squares of the same kind of cloth. Collect five identical indoor/outdoor thermometers. Use masking tape and a marking pen to number these thermometers 1 through 5.
2. Place the thermometers—with the bulb ends

submerged—in a bowl of water that is about 37°C. After five minutes, check and record the temperature of each thermometer.

3. Next, leave thermometer 1 uncovered. Wrap the bulb end of each of the other thermometers with these layers of insulation:

Thermometer 2   one layer
Thermometer 3   two layers
Thermometer 4   three layers
Thermometer 5   four layers

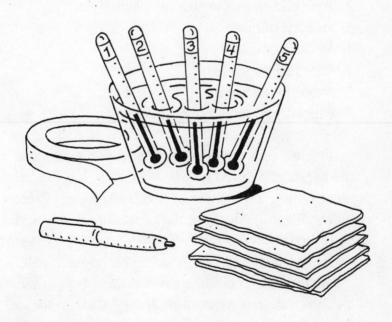

4. Place the five thermometers side by side inside a refrigerator. Wait five minutes. Then, check and record the temperatures.

The manipulated variable in this experiment was the thickness of the insulation. It was changed by adding identical layers of cloth so that the thickness values were zero, one, two, three, and four layers. The responding variable—heat loss—was measured by recording the temperature before and after chilling. These variables were carefully controlled:

1. Type of thermometer
2. Type and size of insulating material
3. Amount of heat
4. Amount of cold
5. Exposure to sunlight
6. Exposure to wind
7. Exposure to moisture in the air

Now, it's your turn to design an experiment. Read the hypothesis stated below. Next, copy the experiment outline on a sheet of notebook paper. Then, fill in the outline to write the procedure that would be followed to perform this experiment. When you've finished, read the solution on pages 47–50.

The hypothesis is: *The more salt there is in water, the lower the temperature must be for the water to freeze.*

Procedure:

1. Manipulated variable
   a. What is the manipulated variable?
   b. What values will you give it—or, in other words, in what ways will you change it?
   c. What materials will you use to do this test?
2. Controlled variables
   a. What variables will you control during this experiment?
   b. What will you do to control these variables?
3. Responding variable
   a. What is the responding variable?
   b. How will you measure the responding variable?

You may word your outline differently, but it will still be correct as long as you present each step clearly. You may want to make a copy of the outline on page 47 and keep it handy. It will guide you anytime you need to design an experiment.

Now, here's the solution:

Procedure:

1. Collect five identical cups. Use a grease pencil or permanent marker to number these cups 1 through 5.

2. Next, pour one-half cup of cold tap water into each cup.

3. Don't add any salt to the first cup. Add salt, in these amounts, to the other four cups:

Cup 2	one-half teaspoon
Cup 3	one teaspoon
Cup 4	one and one-half teaspoons
Cup 5	two teaspoons

4. Stir well. Then, place the five cups side by side in the freezer compartment of a refrigerator. Put an indoor/outdoor thermometer in each cup and close the freezer door.

5. After five minutes, check to see if ice has formed on the surface of the water in any of the cups. Continue to check every five minutes for ice. As soon as ice is present, check and record the temperature of the water in that cup. Once ice has formed, and the temperature has been recorded, disregard that cup and continue checking on the others.

6. Repeat this test two more times.

Did you notice that in this procedure no salt was

added to the first cup of water? Look back at the other sample procedures presented in earlier chapters. In each of them, you'll be able to spot one part of the test that shows what would occur naturally. Scientists call this part of the test the *control*. The control lets you compare the effect of the manipulated variable to the unmanipulated or normal results of exposing an object to a specific set of conditions. It's an important part of any experiment.

When you're designing an experiment and you decide to change the value of the manipulated variable in, for example, four ways, add a fifth setup. Treat these setups exactly the same except for the manipulated variable. And in one of the setups don't change this variable at all. That unmanipulated setup will be your control.

After you've planned the procedure for your experiment, you'll want to make a neat copy of it in the PROCEDURE section of your logbook. And as you design your experiment, you many want to track down more information about your test object. Add a RESEARCH section to your logbook, and in addition to what you find in books, encyclopedias, and magazines, you can write away for free pamphlets, pictures, and publications. Your local librarian will be able to help you find the addresses of public facilities, government agencies, museums, institutions, and zoos that you can write to for information.

You may also want to talk to an expert. Depending on what you choose to investigate, a dentist, a farmer, a chemist, an engineer, or some other person may have experience that could help you do a better job designing your experiment. Adults are usually willing to help—either in finding an expert or in answering your questions—if you're courteous and explain that you're working on a science project. When you do interview an expert, be sure to be brief and limit your questions to the topic at hand.

OK! You've designed an experiment, written down the procedure step-by-step, and you're ready to conduct the test and collect data. But wait! Before you actually start performing any experiments, there's something special you should know. Scientists use six basic skills called *process skills.* These are the *skills* they use in the *process* of doing an experiment. Knowing how to use those skills can help you do your experiment. But here's a secret: You already have these investigative tools; you use them every day! And you can find out what they are, and how to make even better use of them, just by turning the page.

Learning How to Use the Six Basic Science Process Skills

The six basic process skills that a scientist uses while conducting an experiment are: *observing, measuring, classifying, communicating, inferring,* and *predicting.* These are actually skills that you just naturally use. In fact, whenever you go to the ballpark, you use at least some of these skills. For example, you arrive there and one of the things you *observe* is whether or not there are enough people to form two teams on the field. You *communicate* with the others to choose sides. You may *infer,* once the teams are chosen, who has the stronger team from seeing how many good players are on each side. And based on those inferences, you can *predict* the outcome of the game before it's played—perhaps that your team will win! What you probably need to be aware of is how to use these skills in the precise, careful way a scientist does.

Observing means using your senses—sight, hearing, smell, touch, taste—to collect information.

That's how you made your first discoveries about the world. Your senses are still the main way you explore and learn about things. And information you collect through your senses is called *qualitative observations*.

To make qualitative observations the way a scientist would, though, you need to pay really close attention to the messages your sensory organs—eyes, ears, nose, tongue, and skin—receive. You may have noticed that something that was cooking smelled good. But did you try to figure out just what that scent was—apples baking or beef frying? When you experiment, observing will be an especially important skill.

Of course, the best way to learn to use your senses as tools to collect information is to perform an experiment. Keeping in mind that all solids are made of particles, the hypothesis for this experiment is: *The smaller the particles, the faster a solid dissolves.* Collect four bouillon cubes, masking tape, a marking pen, a sheet of waxed paper, a table knife, water, a timer, and four clear plastic cups. Then answer the questions listed with each step; record your observations as you work through the experiment.

Procedure:
1. Unwrap the bouillon cubes and place them on the waxed paper. Describe how the cubes look. How

do they feel? How do they smell? Make your observations as detailed as possible—write down color, texture, size, etc.

2. Use masking tape and a marking pen to number the cups 1 through 4. Next, fill each of the cups half full of lukewarm tap water. Make the water the same temperature in each cup. Put your finger in one cup after the other. Does the water seem to be the same temperature in each cup? If not, describe how much difference you can feel.

3. Set one whole bouillon cube in front of cup 1. With the knife, slice a cube into two pieces and set these in front of cup 2. Slice another cube into quarters and set these in front of cup 3. Crumble the last cube into tiny pieces and place these in front of cup 4. As quickly as possible, add the cube or pieces to the respective cups.

4. Make a chart like the one below with four sections—one for each of the cups—and number these 1 through 4.

Cups	Observations
1	
2	
3	
4	

5. Watch closely. Then write down exactly what you see happening in each cup in its section of the chart. Tell how the bouillon cubes look, smell, and feel at the end of one minute.

As you can see, you have to decide which senses are safe to use (you wouldn't want to *taste* all those salty samples!) and which ones will provide you with useful information when you experiment. Then you need to make careful, detailed observations—using those senses—before, during, and after the test. And of course, if you were doing this experiment for a science project, you would need to repeat this test at least two more times.

Measuring is really an extension of your observational skills because there are times when your senses can't provide you with precise information. For example, you needed to be more precise when you were trying to decide if the water in each cup was the same temperature. On those occasions when your senses aren't enough, you need to use measuring tools, such as a thermometer, a ruler, or a scale, to find out how warm, how big, or how heavy something is. Measurements are also called *quantitative observations,* as opposed to qualitative observations, made by the senses alone. Scientists are careful to collect very precise quantitative observations. They use the metric system because it is used by scientists around the world. If a scientist in another country repeats or alters an experiment, he or she will easily be able to compare the new data to what has already been collected.

Here's a fun experiment that will let you practice making precise metric measurements. The hypothesis is: *The more weight in the nose, the farther a paper airplane will travel*. You'll need some sheets of typing paper, scissors, four large paper clips, a kitchen scale, and a long measuring tape. To get started, prepare four identical test planes following the directions below. Then, as you follow the procedure, record your quantitative observations for each test on a sheet of notebook paper.

How to build a paper airplane.

1. Fold a sheet of typing paper in half lengthwise.
2. Open and fold corners A and B to the center crease.
3. Fold C and D to the crease.
4. Bring the two sides of the plane together to re-fold it lengthwise. And fold down the wings.

Procedure:

1. After the four identical planes have been built, number them 1 through 4.
2. Next, cut twelve identical paper squares. Use one large paper clip to hold these weights on the nose of each plane:

Plane 1   Paper clip only

Plane 2   Paper clip and two paper squares

Plane 3   Paper clip and four paper squares

Plane 4   Paper clip and six paper squares

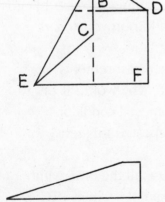

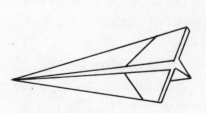

3. If necessary, fold the paper squares so they do not change the shape of the plane's nose section. Then weigh each plane on the kitchen scale. Make a chart like the one shown below and write down the weight of each plane in grams next to its number.

Plane	Distance traveled
1	
2	
3	
4	

4. Find an open area, mark a starting line, and launch each plane in the same way with the same amount of force. Then, use the long measuring tape to find out how many meters and centimeters each plane traveled. Record this information on your chart.

Why would really precise measurements be so important in this experiment? Why would it be important to be sure the environmental conditions were nearly the same when you repeated this test?

Classifying is a skill you use all the time without even thinking about it. For example, when you have a variety of foods to pick from, you automatically classify those foods into two groups—those you want to eat and those you don't.

In order to classify, you need to be able to identify the traits or properties of objects, people, and events. Scientists call these traits or properties *attributes*. In some experiments, classifying helps you select items to be tested. And in others, the results of the experiments you perform direct you to classify the test items in a specific way. In this experiment, you'll be using this skill when you collect your test items and also at the end of the investigation.

The hypothesis of this experiment is: The smaller the spaces between fibers of a paper towel, the faster water travels through it.

To get started, use a magnifying glass to take a close look at a number of different brands of paper towel. Look at and note the size of the spaces between the fibers. Next, select two samples—one with tiny spaces and one with large spaces. You'll also need two quart jars, scissors, two pencils, cellophane tape, a centimeter ruler, water, a measuring cup, a clock or watch with a second hand, and a ballpoint pen. Then, follow the steps in the procedure, taking notes on what happens as you go.

Procedure:

1. Cut three strips, 5 centimeters wide and 25 cen-

timeters long, from each of the two sample paper towels.

2. Pour one cup of water into each jar. Tape the top of a paper-towel strip with small spaces to a pencil. And tape a strip with large spaces to the other pencil.

3. Have a friend help you place each paper-towel strip in a jar at exactly the same time. If necessary, roll the paper on the pencil so that only the bottom edge touches the water.

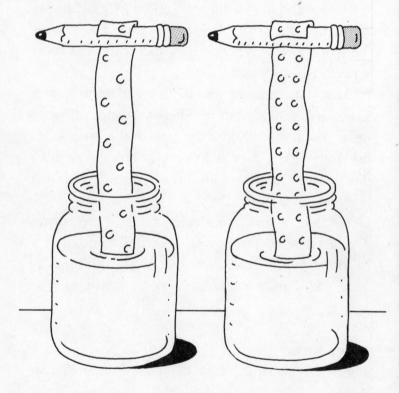

4. The water will move up through the paper towels. Have your friend help you to mark the top of each column of water after exactly ten seconds. The water will keep on going up, but the mark will tell you how far the water traveled during the test time. Measure that distance with the ruler. Make a chart like the one shown below to record the results.

Size of spaces	Distance water traveled in ten seconds		
	Test 1	Test 2	Test 3
Small spaces			
Large spaces			

5. Repeat the test twice and fill in the chart.

Now, use a magnifying glass to check the size of spaces between the fibers in some of the other brands of paper towels you were examining at the beginning of the experiment. Then, classify these towels into two groups—those that absorb quickly and those that don't absorb quickly—based on what you discovered during the test.

Communicating is something you did even before you learned how to talk. When you learned how to speak and then to write, you had a lot of practice using this skill. What you need to learn now is how to communicate the way a scientist does, using precise language and comparative statements. In case that sounds hard, read on! You'll see that it's easy, once you know how.

For example, instead of saying pour *some* water into the jar, you need to say pour *one-half cup* of water into the jar. Or instead of saying that something is *small,* you could make the description more effective by comparing it to something familiar. You could say, for example, not only that it's *small* but that it's *about the size of a quarter.* When you use this kind of language, the directions you present in your experiment's procedure will be clear and easy for others to follow. And the observations you make when you perform the test will provide any reader with accurate information.

To practice your communication skills, write the steps you would need to follow to perform the experiment pictured on the next page.

The hypothesis for this experiment is: *As the amount of sugar increases, the amount of gas given off by the yeast increases.* Check yourself by reading the solution on pages 64 and 65.

Procedure:

To perform this experiment, collect four identical soda-pop bottles, measuring spoons, granulated sugar, four balloons, masking tape, a pen, four packages of dried yeast, a measuring cup, warm water, a 60-centimeter piece of string, and a centimeter ruler. As always, your steps for this procedure may be worded differently, but they will still be correct as long as they express these basic ideas:

1. Use the masking tape to label each bottle, numbers one through four. Pour one-half cup of warm water into each of the four identical soda-pop bottles.

2. Pour or spoon one package of yeast into each bottle.

3. Don't put any sugar into bottle 1. Add a different amount of sugar to each of the other bottles. Add one-half teaspoonful to bottle 2, one teaspoonful to bottle 3, one-and-a-half teaspoonfuls to bottle 4.

4. Cover the mouths of the bottles with identical balloons. Place the bottles in a warm place away from drafts and out of direct sunlight.

5. As soon as the balloons begin to inflate, start to measure each of their diameters at the fattest point. Place one end of the string against the balloon, wrap it around, and pinch the end of the string to mark how much is needed to encircle the balloon. Then lay the string out along the ruler. Check the mea-

surement next to the point marked (this lets you know the diameter of the inflated balloon) and record this information on a chart.

6. Remeasure every fifteen minutes until all of the balloons stop expanding.

7. Repeat the test at least two more times.

Did you include steps 6 and 7 in your list? It's important to record when to stop making observations and taking measurements. In this case, the limit for both is when the balloons stop expanding because this signals that the yeast has stopped releasing gas. The instruction to perform the test at least three times is one that should be included in every experiment's procedure.

What gas does yeast give off? Why does yeast give off gas? You can find the answers to these mysteries at the library. Can you construct another hypothesis that would let you investigate something about yeast growth?

You make an **inference** when you observe something happening and try to explain what may have caused it. For example, you might say that the egg you were frying burned because the pan wasn't greased. That explanation is called an inference.

When you infer the way a scientist would, though, you don't just offer *one* possible explanation. You try to list *every* possible explanation you can think of. You'll probably need to research your test item to help you think of what conditions could have caused the results you observed. That's right—what you're really looking for are variables. After a scientist compiles a list of possible inferences, he or she experiments further, making more observations to test which of these inferences most likely caused the observed results.

Ready to try another experiment? Here's one that uses inference as an investigative tool. First, look at the following picture. One cup of water was poured into each soil-filled funnel. But different amounts of water drained through.

Write down as many inferences as you can think of for why different amounts of water were collected in each jar. Then read on to check yourself.

You may have come up with additional inferences. Don't worry if your inferences are worded differently; they still are correct as long as these ideas are expressed:

1. The water was poured in at different speeds; the faster it was poured, the more water ran through.
2. The water was different temperatures; the warmer the water, the more of it ran through.
3. The soil particles were different sizes; the bigger the particles were, the more water ran through.

You could write a hypothesis and design an experiment to test each of these inferences. What you observed would then help you decide which inference was the best explanation for the results you observed originally.

Predicting is another useful investigative tool when used the way a scientist would. The key to making successful predictions is to learn to recognize patterns, as you'll see in this experiment.

The hypothesis is: *As the amount of water in a container increases, the pitch (highness) of the sound produced by striking the container decreases.*

Start by collecting six identical quart jars, masking tape, a marking pen, water, a metal spoon, and a measuring cup. Then follow these steps:

Procedure:

1. Line the jars up in a row. Put a strip of tape on each jar. And number the jars 1 through 6.

2. Add the following amount of water to each jar:

Jar 1	one-half cup
Jar 2	one cup
Jar 3	one and one-half cups
Jar 4	two cups
Jar 5	two and one-half cups
Jar 6	three cups

3. Strike the side of jar 1 with the metal spoon and listen. Next, strike jars 2, 3, and 4 in order. Don't strike jars 5 and 6.

You probably noticed that as the amount of water in the jar increased, the sound you heard when you struck the jar was lower. Based on this pattern, you can accurately predict whether jar 5 will produce a higher or lower sound than jar 4. And you can make a similar prediction about jar 6. Even more important, you can decide whether the hypothesis you tested is true or false. All this because you recognized what is called a pattern.

OK—you now have a whole set of skills to use as investigative tools. And you've had a lot of practice designing experiments. So you're probably eager to conduct an experiment. That's coming up—next.

How to Conduct an Experiment

So far, you've only gotten ready to do an experiment by learning about other experiments. Now it's time to conduct your own from beginning to end.

The first thing you need to do when you're conducting an experiment is to decide where you will work. You will also need to choose materials and equipment.

A science laboratory is equipped with measuring instruments, electricity, heating and cooling appliances, running water, a supply of chemicals, and plenty of work space. Practically everything you'll need to conduct your experiments can be found here.

Are you thinking that this science laboratory sounds remarkably like a kitchen? That's exactly the point—your lab *is* a kitchen. You'll probably need permission to work there, and the person who runs your "home laboratory" may want to supervise the use of certain equipment. Like a good scientist, when you've finished experimenting, you'll also want to clean up the lab.

Now, let's get to work on the experiment you already designed in step 5. The hypothesis for that experiment is: *The more salt there is in water, the lower the temperature must be for the water to freeze.*

And here, once again, are the variables and the procedure set up to test the relationship between the manipulated and responding variables.

Manipulated variable: salt (values—zero, one-half teaspoon, one teaspoon, one and one-half teaspoons, and two teaspoons)

Responding variable: temperature at which ice first forms

Controlled variables:

size and shape of the container	amount of water
exposure to sunlight	exposure to moving air
air temperature	exposure to moisture in the air
type of thermometer	temperature of water at the start

Procedure:

1. Collect five identical cups. Use a grease pencil

71

or a permanent marker to number these cups 1 through 5.

2. Next, pour one-half cup of tap water into each cup.

3. Don't add any salt to the first cup. Add salt, in these amounts, to the other four cups.

Cup 2	one-half teaspoon
Cup 3	one teaspoon
Cup 4	one and one-half teaspoons
Cup 5	two teaspoons

4. Stir well. Then place the five cups side by side in the freezer compartment of a refrigerator. Put an indoor/outdoor thermometer in each cup and close the freezer door.

5. After five minutes, check to see if ice has formed on the surface of the water in any of the cups. Continue to check every five minutes for ice. As soon as ice is present, check and record the temperature of the water in that cup.

6. Repeat this test two times.

This procedure is what you've planned to do. Now, you need to decide exactly what equipment and materials you're going to use to carry out the experiment. Make a list and keep in mind things you already have on hand. You want to keep your experiment as inexpensive as possible to perform and repeat. Find out what household materials you are allowed to use and also those supplies or equipment that will be safe for you to use.

For this experiment you'll need:

1. salt (From the pantry or buy some at the store—it's cheap.)
2. five identical cups (Clear plastic ones might be the best choice; these are not expensive.)
3. a grease pencil or permanent marker (If you decide to use a marker, you'll probably want to change step 1 to read: Put a strip of masking tape on each cup and use a marker to number these 1 through 5.)
4. a measuring spoon and measuring cup (These should be in the kitchen.)
5. water (Always available on tap.)
6. a freezer (You may need to clear a space in the freezer section of your refrigerator; get permission, no matter what.)
7. five indoor-outdoor thermometers (Don't buy these; try to borrow them from your school or local high school.)

Next, use this list to collect the supplies you need. Once you have everything together, you'll be ready to conduct your experiment.

But don't start yet! What are you going to do with the results? You need to prepare an organized, efficient way to record the information you collect. A data table is your best bet.

When you construct a data table, you divide a piece of paper into columns—one for the manipulated variable on the left and one for the responding variable on the right. Then, you list the values of the manipulated variable in its column. You'll write down the values of the responding variable as you perform the experiment.

Here is a data table for the sample experiment:

Amount of dissolved salt	Freezing temperature of water
0 teaspoons	
½ teaspoon	
1 teaspoon	
1½ teaspoons	
2 teaspoons	

Or if you want to use the same table to collect data from a number of tests, you could set it up this way:

74

Amount of
dissolved salt   Freezing temperature of water

	Test 1	Test 2	Test 3	Average
0 teaspoon				
½ teaspoon				
1 teaspoon				
1½ teaspoons				
2 teaspoons				

As you can see, this data table also includes a column for recording the *average* results. While it's necessary to repeat the tests to see if the results are the same or nearly the same every time, multiple sets of results can make looking for a relationship between the manipulating and responding variables difficult. Averaging the results simplifies the comparison.

To compute an average, you just total all the numbers that represent the same data. Then, you divide this sum by how many pieces of data you just added up. For example, let's say that these were the freezing temperatures for the cup with 2 teaspoons of salt added:

$$-4°C$$
$$-6°C$$
$$-5°C$$

When you add up these three numbers, the total is $-15°C$. Then you divide that sum by three since that's how many numbers were added up. So in this case, the average freezing temperatures for water with 2 teaspoons is $-5°C$.

Now, it's your turn. On a sheet of notebook paper, construct a data table for each of these sets of variables. Remember, each test will need to be conducted three times. When you've finished, check the solutions.

1. *Manipulated variable*: number of coils (10, 20, 30)
   Responding variable: number of paper clips picked up
2. *Manipulating variable*: amount of fertilizer (0, ½, 1, 1½, 2 teaspoons)
   Responding variable: height of plant

1. Number
of coils   Number of paper clips picked up

	Test 1	Test 2	Test 3	Average
10				
20				
30				

2. Amount
of fertilizer   Height of plants

	Test 1	Test 2	Test 3	Average
0 teaspoon				
½ teaspoon				
1 teaspoon				
1½ teaspoons				
2 teaspoons				

Your data table should be included in your logbook. On your OBSERVATION page, record both qualitative and quantitative observations of what happens.

While a data table can help you determine the relationship between the manipulated and responding variable, a graph can make the job even easier. You've probably heard the old saying "A picture's worth a thousand words." Well, a graph is a kind of picture.

A graph is a grid of lines running horizontally and vertically on the page. The graph on the next page presents some fictional results for the sample experiment. Notice that the manipulated variable's values are shown along the *horizontal line* (also called the *horizontal axis*), which runs from left to right. And what is called the scale for the responding variable is shown along the *vertical line* (also called the *vertical axis*), which runs from bottom to top. This is a rule you should follow when you construct a graph for your experiment.

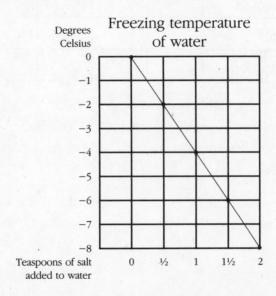

Freezing temperature of water

To find out what any specific responding variable is on this graph, place an index finger on the value of the manipulated variable you want to know. Let's say you want to know at what temperature ice first formed when the water contained one-half teaspoon of salt. Follow the vertical line straight up from the one-half teaspoon mark to the X.

Then, while hold your right index finger on that $X,$ run the index finger of your left hand sideways to the left until you reach the responding-variable scale. That point on the scale is the average freezing temperature for water containing one-half teaspoon of salt.

Remember, that graph was plotted with fictional results. To actually record a responding variable for a specific value of a manipulated variable, follow these directions: First, place one index finger on the point on the responding-variable scale you need to record. Then, place your other index finger on the manipulated-variable value for which you want to record the results. Move your first finger sideways to the right and your other finger straight up until your two index fingers meet. And make an X at the point where your fingers meet. (Be sure, of course, to quickly check that one of your fingers has not overshot the correct spot.)

Look back at the fictional graph. A graph is useful because it neatly shows the relationship between the manipulated and responding variables. The diagonal line formed by connecting all the *X*s reveals at a glance that as the amount of salt in the water increased, the freezing temperature decreased.

Instead of a line graph, you could make a bar graph to present this same pattern. You simply find the point where the two lines intersect as before, only instead of making an *X,* you color a column from the manipulated variable's value up to the level on the responding variable's scale that represents the results. The advantage of a bar graph is that the wide-colored bars will show up better than a thin line on your project's display.

Now that you know how to experiment, record the data you collect, and average the results, you'll want to actually *perform* the experiment. How does the amount of salt affect the freezing temperature of water?

After you look at the graph you make of your results, turn to the CONCLUSION section of your logbook. State what relationship you observed between the manipulated and responding variables and whether this proves that the hypothesis you constructed is true or false. If your experiment proves that your hypothesis is false, it's a good idea to suggest another hypothesis that you infer might be true and could be tested.

You're probably thinking, "Isn't it possible that

something could go wrong when I perform my experiment? What if I can't collect any data—then what?"

Don't panic. It's always possible that your test may not go the way you expected. The seeds you plant might rot instead of sprout. Or maybe the electromagnet you construct won't attract any paper clips. Actually, scientists consider mistakes just part of the process.

First, try to identify any variables that might be causing you problems—possibly variables you forgot to control. Are the seeds too old to sprout? Or could the battery you used for your electromagnet be dead? Start early and allow yourself plenty of time to experiment. Then, if you have problems, there's time to start over with new materials (seeds, batteries, or whatever) or new ideas.

Of course, it's possible that your results will never be what you expect. For example, Sir Alexander Fleming was testing how a certain variable affected bacteria growth. One day, he discovered that mold had contaminated the bacteria he was growing. Dr. Fleming was about to throw away the sample and start over when he noticed that the mold had actually killed the bacteria wherever it came into contact with it.

Dr. Fleming investigated the mold. And in later experiments, he proved that a substance from this mold could be used to cure people of some diseases caused by bacteria. This mold was penicillin. It was the first antibiotic. And because it saved so many lives, penicillin became known as the "wonder drug."

You probably won't always be able to turn an unexpected result into such a dramatic success. But the point is that experiments don't really *fail*. Make careful qualitative and quantitative observations. Then, if your experiment doesn't go the way you thought it would, tell what *did* happen when you write your conclusion. Explain *why* you think this happened and suggest how you would further test this inference.

OK—you're finally ready to do what you wanted to do when you started reading this book. So what are you going to do for your science project?

STEP 8

Choosing a Project

Deciding what you're going to investigate may seem like the toughest part of doing a science project. But, fortunately, there are four things you can do to find a terrific project idea.

1. Check out commercial claims. Just spend an hour or two watching TV, paying special attention to commercial breaks, and take notes. Don't hesitate to shout: "Oh, sure!" as you get into the spirit of things. And you'll discover a wide range of possible experiments perfect for a science project. For example, does one battery really outlast all the others? Does one brand of detergent actually remove stains better than other brands do? Does one brand of detergent actually clean as well in cold water as it does in hot? Does one brand of paper towel absorb more water than another does? Or, for that matter, can one brand of paper towel absorb water faster than *any* others do?

Sometimes, you will have to think up your own experiment to test a commercial claim. Other times, you may want to duplicate a test you've seen on TV to see if you get the same results. For example, one antacid commercial shows the tablets being dropped into a foamy glass of beer. Later, the beer is shown with the foam gone because the antacid has eliminated the gas. Would that really happen? How quickly?

2. Test familiar practices. There are some things you've probably learned to do because your parents always do them. Your parents learned these useful techniques from *their* parents. For example, does your dad always try to promptly touch up a spot of chipped paint on your family car? Or does your mom sprinkle a little lemon juice or orange juice on freshly peeled and sliced apples to keep them from turning dark? You could see what happens to metal if it's left exposed to the weather. Or you could find out how long the citrus juice protects the apples. You could even do a more in-depth study, trying to find out (by using vitamin C tablets dissolved in distilled water) if it's the vitamin C in the citrus juice that prevents the fruit from turning dark. You might explore why the drying process preserves food, why people cover plants when the weather turns frosty, or why they crumble eggshell into the soil of a flowerpot.

3. Try to improve on something. Or, find a problem that needs to be solved. Doing this kind of science project can turn you into an inventor. For example, Thomas A. Edison wasn't the first person to invent an incandescent light bulb. But the earliest bulbs only glowed for a few seconds before the filaments melted. What Edison did was experiment and experiment to find a better filament material. He wanted to find something that would glow brightly, but only burn itself up slowly. Like all good scientists, Edison kept a record of his observations as he experimented. And he filled more than forty thousand pages with notes before he discovered a filament that glowed for more than 100 hours.

You probably won't patent the results of your science project. But let your imagination go! Think of something you could try to improve. Could something other than rubber be used to erase mistakes on paper but not wear out so quickly? Is there a better design for the closure strip that keeps self-sealing plastic bags zipped shut? Or is there a plant that doesn't need mowing that could be used along roadsides to prevent erosion?

4. Look for cause-and-effect relationships. Go exploring around your home and in your neighborhood. Look for something out of the ordinary, such as a spot of lawn where the grass is thicker and lusher than anywhere else. Next, make a list of all the inferences that might explain what has caused this. Then, read about grass and plant growth and select the inference you think is most likely. Your science project could test that inference.

Or look for something that has changed, such as a rake that was left outdoors and became rusty. List all the variables that could have caused that change. Then, read about metal and rust and select one variable to test. For your science project, you could design an experiment to find out the relationship between that variable and rust formation.

You could also go on an exploring trip to the

library. Search through books about a topic that particularly interests you, maybe airplanes. As you find out more about this special topic, think about cause-and-effect relationships you might investigate. For example, does the height of the tail fin effect a plane's stability? You could devise an experiment that tests your hypothesis.

Once you find a *topic* that interests you, the next step is to ensure that the topic would make a suitable *science project* for you. Ask yourself these questions.

1. *Does the experiment you're planning fit your school's rules?*

In many school systems, you have to have special permission to use certain materials, such as microorganisms (like bacteria or fungi) and tissue samples (like blood, bone, or hair). There may also be rules about using animal or human subjects. These requirements are made so that experiments will be done safely, and with respect for living things. They're also designed to make sure the materials you use don't make you sick.

By finding out about any limitations before you pick a project, you'll avoid problems later. But even if your school doesn't have any specific rules against

87

it, please don't pick an experiment that uses animals or human subjects. Those kinds of experiments are best left to experienced, professional scientists.

2. *How hard will the experiment be?*

It's boring to stand around watching someone else experiment. And having to wait for an adult to help can leave you feeling confused and frustrated; you want to do your experiment without depending on anyone else. So pick a science project that you'll be able to do by yourself.

3. *Will you have enough time to finish?*

If your teacher has assigned a science project to you, or if you're planning to enter a science fair and you've got a deadline, plan ahead; try to estimate how much time you need. A project that requires you to experiment with growing plants, for example, will probably take more time than one testing an electromagnet. Don't forget you'll also need some time at the end to prepare a display.

When you decide what you will investigate for your science project, write your topic as a question. Scientists call this question the project's *purpose*. By stating your topic as a question, you give your investigation a purpose—finding an answer.

To write your science project's purpose, you'll first

need to decide either what responding variable you'll be measuring or what manipulated variable you'll be controlling. If you start with the responding variable, your question will ask what affects this variable. For example, if you're going to measure germination (seeds sprouting), your project's purposes would be: *What affects germination?* The word *affect* is often used when writing the science project's purpose because it indicates that you're looking for something—you're not sure what—that will influence that responding variable. On the other hand, if you start with the manipulating variable, your question would ask what effect this variable would have. For example, if you want to design a new wing shape for a paper airplane, your project's purpose would be: *How will changing a paper airplane's wing shape affect its flight?*

After you've written your project's purpose, the next step is to construct a hypothesis. Look at step 4 if you need to. Then think about the experiment you'll need to do to test this hypothesis. As soon as you've decided what experiment you'll perform, write your purpose and hypothesis in your logbook. This officially launches your science project! Look back through steps 3 through 7 for guidance as you prepare to experiment, conduct the test, collect and analyze the results, and write your conclusion.

You will probably want to include a written report with your science project to tell about your experiment and to share any interesting background information you discovered while you researched your topic. A written report may even be required. In either case, you are ready for step 9. It has directions to help you write a super report.

Preparing a Written Report

The report you write for your science project will have two parts—the section that tells how you set up your experiment and what you discovered, and the section that explains what you learned as you researched your topic. Before you start writing, you need to organize your material.

The information about your experiment is already in order because you planned, set up, and conducted this test in an organized way. Your research material, though, may need to be collected and sorted. Start by making a list of the questions you tried to answer as you read and talked to experts. Leave room below each question for the answers you found. You may have discovered conflicting answers. List all of these; you'll want to report all sides of an issue. When you've finished, look back through your questions and answers. Number the questions in the order you'll want to present the information in your report. Try to decide if there is a logical order to the information. Ask yourself: "Would knowing one thing help make explaining something else later on easier?" If the answer is yes, then that information must come early in your report.

Ready to write? Here are some general writing tips you'll want to keep in mind:

1. *Start each paragraph with a topic sentence.* A topic sentence summarizes what you'll explain in that paragraph. Then each sentence within the paragraph provides details to help illustrate and explain the topic sentence.
2. *Indent the beginning of each paragraph.*
3. *Begin each sentence with a capital letter.*
4. *End each sentence with a period, a question mark, or an exclamation mark.*

Begin the section of your report that discusses your experiment by writing your project's hypothesis at the top of the page. Then, using your procedure as a guide, write sentences that describe how you set up your experiment and what you did, step-by-step. Check the observations you recorded as you conducted the experiment. Then, describe in your report what you observed. Include plenty of details and use comparative phrases to communicate your results clearly. You may want to include photographs, drawings, or even a copy of your chart or graph to further illustrate what you are explaining. Finally, tell how you analyzed the results. And write out your conclusions.

Begin the research section of your report by changing the question you designated as number 1 to a topic sentence. Next, read through the answers you listed below this question. Write sentences that present those answers. Then, go on to question 2; make it a statement and start a new paragraph. Write as you did for question 1.

When you've finished writing up your research, your report is complete. But it isn't ready to present. This is only a rough draft. You'll need to revise it. Don't be in a hurry and skip this step. Even professional writers spend time revising what they write to improve it. In order to fine-tune your report, read back through it and follow these steps:

1. *Check for any important facts or details you may have left out.* If you find something that needs to be included, write it above the point where you

want to insert it. Or write it in the margin and draw an arrow to the point in the report where it needs to be added.

2. *Cross out any words or phrases that aren't needed.*
3. *Change any words that don't sound quite right.*

After you've made these changes, read the revised report aloud to yourself or to someone else. Listen to what you're saying. And ask yourself: "Does what I've written tell clearly what I want to say?" If not, you'll want to do some more revising. Perhaps you need to add more sentences to explain your topic sentences. Or maybe the order in which you present your material needs to be changed.

When you're satisfied with what you've written, read through your report one more time, checking these points:

1. *Be sure all your sentences are complete sentences, and be sure none of them are run-on.*
2. *Be sure everything is spelled correctly.*
3. *Be sure you've used proper punctuation.*

The last step is to rewrite your report so that it looks attractive. Use your very best handwriting. Your teacher may require you to write your report in pencil or pen or to skip a certain number of lines between lines. Find out any special requirements in advance.

You'll also want to include a *bibliography,* or a list of the books, magazines, or other sources you used. Write the word BIBLIOGRAPHY at the top of a clean sheet of paper. Use the first word of each entry, and organize the list in alphabetical order. Your teacher may have a special format for you to use; if not, here are general rules and examples you can follow. Notice that the first line of each entry is not indented, while all the additional lines are. And pay close attention to the punctuation.

Encyclopedia: List the article title (if one's given) or the topic, the name of the encyclopedia, and the publication date.

"Plants." *World Book.* 1988.

Book: List the author (last name first), the title, the publisher's location, the publisher, and the most recent date the book was published (you may want to ask an adult to help you figure this out).

Selsam, Millicent E. *Play with Seeds.* New York: William Morrow and Company, 1957.

Magazine: Give the author (last name first) if one is listed, the title of the article, the name of the publication, the volume number (if shown), the publication date, and the pages where the article appeared.

Algozin, Mary. "And You Thought It Was a Dipper!" *Odyssey* 9, no. 3 (March 1987): 4–9.

Newspaper: List the author (last name first) if one is given, the title of the article, the name of the newspaper, the date published, the section number (if included), and the pages where the article was found.

Jeffers, Tom, "Fabulous Fakes," *The New York Times,* June 21, 1987, IV: p 25.

Interview: List the person's name (last name first), his or her title, and the company, university, or agency where employed.

Madison, Steven, director of Public Relations. Edison Historical Site Museum.

When you've finished, carefully stack the pages of your report in order with the bibliography last. Add colored sheets of construction paper for the front and back covers, put your name and the title of your science project on the front, and staple your report along the left edge.

And now for the second part of doing a science project. You've got to let the world know about your experiment.

You could prepare a TV program about your experiment. Or you could put up a giant billboard. You could even have the Goodyear blimp flash messages about it in lights. Who knows? Maybe someday you *will* tell the story of an experiment you perform in one of those ways. But for now, something a little simpler—and a lot less expensive—will do the job very nicely. How to tell the story of your experiment is coming up—step 10.

Preparing the Display

Would a title like that grab your attention? You bet it would—especially if the black letters were printed on a bright yellow-and-red background. You would have to take a closer look. You'd want to find out just what was rotten about that project. In this case, the title is just a clever, eye-catching way of announcing that the experiment tested how temperature affected mold growth. But that's just what you need to get started—a title that will make people come closer and look at your project.

Preparing the Display

Once you've gotten people interested, your display should hold their attention. First, figure out some way to get your material up at eye level where it's easy to read. And give it impact—bright colors, bold letters, and lots of pictures.

Freestanding panels are a good way to display your work. You may want to use two or three panels, depending on how much material you need to present. And as you can see, there's plenty of room for creativity.

99

You could make your display panels out of corrugated cardboard or triwall cardboard, the kind used in sturdy boxes. Art-supply stores also carry several types of stiff cardboard. You'll need to hook these separate panels together with strong tape so they'll stand up by themselves. If you want cardboard panels that are already hooked together, check stores that sell sewing supplies for a cardboard cutting board. It will be too tall, but you can easily trim it down to a size suitable for displaying the project.

If you want something you can use this year, next year, and the year after that, make your display panels out of wood. Plywood, pegboard, and particleboard panels work well and can be hooked together with metal hinges. You will probably need an adult's help.

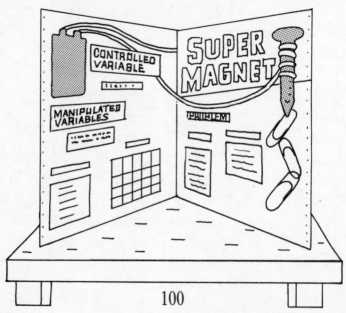

Wondering how big to make your display? It may be up to you. Then the sky is the limit. If, however, you're preparing your project for a science fair, your teacher should give you specific measurements. Check what's required before you start constructing the display. Here are the measurements set by the International Science and Engineering Fair:

width	80 centimeters
height	270 centimeters from the floor
depth	75 centimeters

If there is a height limitation "from the floor" and your project will be sitting on a table, you'll need to take the table's height into consideration. For example, let's say the height of the table is 75 centimeters. If the height of the display panels is 125 centimeters, the project's height is the *total* of these two measurements: 200 centimeters.

If your panels aren't already colored, you'll want to color them. You can use contact paper, paint, felt, or cloth stretched tightly over each panel and taped or stapled to the back. Use a bright, solid color, such as red, blue, yellow, or green, which will make your labels and materials stand out.

Whatever the size, shape, and color of your display, the most important thing is to present the story of your experiment in a well-organized way. Per-

haps you can make one panel the "main line," showing the major elements of your experiment.

The additional panels can be used to show the data tables and the graph of your results, plus any background information you may have room to include. You can also use the space immediately in front of your panels. Your logbook needs to be included with your display; this is a good spot for it.

Be creative! Mount lists of information on sheets of colored paper to make them more eye-catching. Use colored lines to connect the points on your graph. Or, if you make a bar graph, color each bar a bright color. For impact and readability, use stencils and marking pens to make headings and labels. Or, if you have access to a computer and a word processing program, print out these headings and labels. Include photos or drawings of different stages of your experiment. Make a model of your test item and label the parts. Or set up a demonstration of how your experiment looked in progress. What you do to make your science project interesting and appealing is limited only by what you can imagine.

When your display is complete, your science project is ready to be turned in. Your display tells the story of what you did and what you discovered. It also shows how carefully and how hard you worked. This is a science project you can be proud to show off. In fact, if you're planning to show it off, you won't want to miss the next chapter. It's all about participating in a science fair.

STEP 11

Being in a Science Fair

Has your teacher suggested that you enter your project in the school science fair? You may be worried, wondering what it will be like. Relax! Science fairs are competitive, but they're also fun. In most science fairs, you aren't present during the judging. You set up your display and leave. Then, when you come back later, if you've won an award, you'll find a ribbon hanging on your display. You might even get "best of show" and be invited to go on to a district or regional science fair.

The judges are usually science teachers from other schools or people from the community who have science-related careers. They are qualified to evaluate the research and investigate what you've done. Most schools provide a point value list for judges to use in scoring each project. While lists differ, projects are usually judged on these points:

Creativity
Scientific method
Thoroughness
Appearance

Judges usually have a lot of projects to evaluate at a science fair; it would take many hours to score them all. So judging teams often split up to take a fast first look at all the projects. Based on an initial impression, each judge "flags" with a strip of colored paper those projects he or she wants to look at more closely. Only those projects receiving more than one flag are actually scored. This may not seem fair, but this process allows judges to spend the time necessary to make a thorough evaluation of those projects that seem to be the best. You've probably already guessed that appearance really counts in having your project become one of the finalists.

At some science fairs, part of being judged is answering questions. Does that thought make you shake in your shoes? Don't worry! By now, you know your project well enough to be able to talk about it easily. Just to make you more comfortable, read back through your logbook and your written report. Then the details will be fresh in your mind. And if it makes you feel even better to have those facts close at hand, you may want to write some notes on index cards.

When it's your turn to be judged, stand up straight next to your display so you won't block anyone's view of the work. Speak clearly. And don't be in a hurry.

One thing that can put you at ease is to have a practice run. Make a list of five or six questions you think the judges might ask you about your project. Think about how you'll respond. And think of those parts of the display you'll point to as you describe the work. Then, ask a parent or a friend to pretend to be a judge and ask you those questions.

Even if no one can practice with you, take time to go over your responses out loud. You may think this is a little foolish. But it isn't. The experience of answering questions about your project will help you gain confidence. And the more sure of yourself you are, the better job you'll do at the science fair. *Good luck. And have fun!*

A BONUS:

Some Suggestions for Possible Projects

Here is a list of questions, divided by topics, that you might choose to be the *purpose* of your science project. Of course, there are lots of other possibilities.

Chemistry
How do food additives affect food?
Does soap affect water's surface tension?
Does temperature affect the vitamin C content of fruit juices?
Do mordants (chemical fixatives) increase the effectiveness of natural dyes?
What affects glue's stickiness?
What affects how well toothpaste removes denture stains?
Does water temperature affect how well detergents remove stains?
What affects rust formation?
What affects how quickly materials dissolve?

Earth science

What affects how quickly water deposits sediments?

What affects erosion?

What affects crystal formation?

What affects surface temperature?

What affects frost formation?

What affects evaporation?

Does soil particle size affect the flow of ground-water?

What affects the acidity of rainwater?

What affects the fertility of the soil?

Physical science

How does wing shape affect an airplane's flight?

Do flaps increase an airplane wing's lifting power?

What affects an airplane's speed?

How does streamlining affect how efficiently a car uses gas?

What affects friction?

What affects a suspension bridge's load-bearing ability?

Does insulation affect a house's internal temperature?

What affects how well a paper towel absorbs water?

What affects an electromagnet's strength?

Plants

Does temperature affect mold growth?

What affects germination?

What affects plant growth?

Does sugar affect yeast growth?

Does wind speed affect how quickly grapes change to raisins?

What affects how many duds are in a batch of popcorn?

What affects how much rubber can stretch?

What affects plant decomposition (rotting)?

Index